Roger McGough is the biggest-selling and most popular poet in Britain. He was one of the Liverpool Poets in the 1960s and since then has published over twenty-five books, including eighteen for children. He now lives in London and tours the country doing hugely entertaining readings and workshops.

Praise for Roger McGough

'A word juggler who never misses a catch'
Charles Causley

'The patron saint of poetry'
Carol Ann Duffy

'He is a true original and more than one generation would be much the poorer without him'
The Times

SENSATIONAL!

POEMS CHOSEN BY ROGER McGOUGH

ILLUSTRATED BY SARA FANELLI

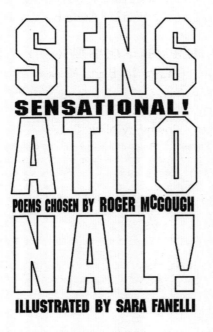

MACMILLAN CHILDREN'S BOOKS

First published 2004 by Macmillan Children's Books

This edition published 2005 by Macmillan Children's Books
a division of Macmillan Publishers Limited
20 New Wharf Road, London N1 9RR
Basingstoke and Oxford
www.panmacmillan.com

Associated companies throughout the world

ISBN: 978-0-330-41344-2

3 5 7 9 8 6 4

A CIP catalogue record for this book is available from the British Library.

Printed and bound in Great Britain by Mackays of Chatham plc, Kent

Researched by Hilary McGough.

CONTENTS

THE SENSES

SIGHT

SOUND

TOUCH

SMELL

TASTE

THE SENSES

THE MAGIC OF THE BRAIN

Such a sight I saw:
An eight-sided kite surging up into a cloud
Its eight tails streaming out as if they were one.
It lifted my heart as starlight lifts the head
Such a sight I saw.

And such a sound I heard.
One bird through dim winter light as the day was closing
Poured out a song suddenly from an empty tree.
It cleared my head as water refreshes the skin
Such a sound I heard.

Such a smell I smelled:
A mixture of roses and coffee, of green leaf and warmth.
It took me to gardens and summer and cities abroad,
Memories of meetings as if my past friends were here
Such a smell I smelled.

Such a soft fur I felt.
It wrapped me around, soothing my winter-cracked skin,
Not gritty or stringy or sweaty but silkily warm
As my animal slept on my lap, and we both breathed content
Such soft fur I felt.

Such food I tasted:
Smooth-on-tongue-soup, and juicy crackling of meat,
Greens like fresh fields, sweet-on-your-palate peas,
Jellies and puddings and fragrance of fruit they are made from
Such good food I tasted.

Such a world comes in:
Far world of the sky to breathe in through your nose
Near world you feel underfoot as you walk on the land.
Through your eyes and your ears and your mouth and your brilliant brain
Such a world comes in.

Jenny Joseph

ANOTHER SENSATIONAL DAY

The roar of parents,
A curse of clocks;
Tinkle of toilets,
Shrugging on socks.

The flop of cereal,
Pop song of toast;
Hurdling buses,
The bell's mad boast.

The jam of lessons,
As hours overtake;
The theft of daydreams,
The scent of break.

A rush-hour of shoes,
The dawdle of light,
A gaggle of gossip
Summoning night.

Excuses for homework,
The glue of the box,
A sinking of pillows . . .

The curse of clocks.

Andrew Fusek Peters

5

I BIT AN APPLE

I bit an apple and the flesh was sweet:
Juice tingled on the tongue and from the fruit
Arose a scent that memory received
And in a flash raised ghosts of apple trees,
Leaves blistered with minutest bulbs of rain
Bewildering an autumn drawing room
Where carpets stained with unaccustomed shadow
Heard one old table creak, perhaps moved too
By some remembrance of a former time
When summer, like a lover, came to him
And laid amazing offerings at his feet.
I bit an apple and the spell was sweet.

Vernon Scannell

NOT ONLY

Not only the leaf shivering with delight
No,
Not only the morning grass shrugging off the weight of frost
No,
Not only the wings of the crane fly consumed by fire
No,
Not only the stream rising from the horse's back
No,
Not only the sound of the sunflower roaring
No,
Not only the golden spider spinning
No,
Not only the cathedral window deep inside the raindrop
No,
Not only the door opening at the back of the clouds
No,
Not only flakes of light settling like snow
No,
Not only the sky as blue and smooth as an egg
No,
Not only these things

Brian Patten

BENEDICTION

Thanks to the ear
that someone may hear

Thanks to seeing
that someone may see

Thanks to feeling
that someone may feel

Thanks to touch
that one may be touched

Thanks to flowering of white moon
and spreading shawl of black night
holding villages and cities together

James Berry

THE DISTANCE

Over the sounding sea,
Off the wandering sea
I smelt the smell of the distance
And longed for another existence.
Smell of pineapple, maize, and myrrh,
Parrot-feather and monkey-fur,
   Brown spice,
   Blue ice,
Fields of tobacco and tea and rice,

And soundless snows,
And snowy cotton,
Otto of rose
Incense in an ivory palace,
Jungle rivers rich and rotten,
   Slumbering valleys
   Smouldering mountains
   Rank morasses
   And frozen fountains,
Black molasses and purple wine,
Coral and pearl and tar and brine,
The smell of panther and polar-bear
   And leopard-lair
   And mermaid-hair
Came from the four-cornered distance,
And I longed for another existence.

Eleanor Farjeon

9

THE OLDEST GIRL IN THE WORLD

Children, I remember how I could hear
with my soft young ears
the tiny sounds of the air –
tinkles and chimes
like minuscule bells
ringing continually there;
clinks and chinks
like glasses of sparky gooseberry wine,
jolly and glinting and raised in the air.
Yes, I could hear like a bat. And how!
Can't hear a sniff of it now.

Truly, believe me, I could all the time see
every insect that crawled in a bush,
every bird that hid in a tree,
individually.
If I wanted to catch a caterpillar
to keep as a pet in a box
I had only to watch a cabbage
and there it would be
crawling bendy and green towards me.
Yes, I could see with the eyes of a cat. Miaow!
Can't see a sniff of it now.

And my sense of taste was second to none,
By God, the amount I knew with my tongue!
The shrewd taste of a walnut's brain.
The taste of a train from a bridge.
Of a kiss. Of air chewy with midge.
Of fudge from a factory two miles away
from the house where I lived.
I'd stick out my tongue
to savour these in a droplet of rain.
Yes, I could taste like the fang of a snake. Wow!
Can't taste a sniff of it now.

On the scent, what couldn't I smell
with my delicate nose, my nostrils of pearl?
I could smell the world!
Snow. Soot. Soil.
Satsumas snug in their Christmas sock.
The ink of a pen.
The stink of an elephant's skin.
The blue broth of a swimming pool. Dive in!
The showbizzy gasp of the wind.
Yes, I could smell like a copper's dog Bow-wow!
Can't smell a sniff of it now.

As for my sense of touch
it was too much!
The cold of a snowball
felt through the vanishing heat of a mitt.
A peach like an apple wearing a vest.
The empty dish of a bird's nest.
A hot chestnut
branding the palm at the heart of the fist.
The stab of the thorn on the rose. Long grass, its itch.
Yes, I could feel with the sensitive hand of a ghost. Whooo!
Can't feel a sniff of it now.

Can't see a
Can't hear a
Can't taste a
Can't smell a
Can't feel a bit of it whiff of it sniff of it.
Can't get a sniff of it now.

Carol Ann Duffy

LEISURE

What is this life if, full of care,
We have no time to stand and stare.

No time to stand beneath the boughs
And stare as long as sheep or cows.

No time to see, when woods we pass,
Where squirrels hide their nuts and grass.

No time to see, in broad daylight,
Streams full of stars like skies at night.

No time to turn at Beauty's glance,
And watch her feet, how they can dance.

No time to wait till her mouth can
Enrich that smile her eyes began

A poor life this if, full of care,
We have no time to stand and stare.

W. H. Davies

FINDING MAGIC

Magic's not that stuff on telly,
we all know how that's done.
No, it's the shimmering pink horizon
at the rising of the sun.

It's not some trick with rabbits
popping from a black top hat
No, it's the furry liquefaction
of a sleekly moving cat.

You can keep disappearing elephants
worked by reflective glass
look instead at daisies
prinking in the glass.

Sawing the lady in pieces
or making her disappear
is nothing to the moonlight
reflected in the mere.

There's no trick anywhere like it
nor a more impressive sight
than when the winter's icy wand
magics everywhere snow white

So never mind the conjurer
as he tries to trick your view
think about nature's cleverest trick
that most appeals to you!

Angela Topping

SENSING MOTHER

Dad keeps Mum's favourite dress
deep in the bottom of the ottoman.
Sometimes, when he is at work
I stand listening to the tick of the clock
then go upstairs.

And propping up
the squeaky wooden lid, I dig through
layers of rough, winter blankets
feeling for that touch of silk.
The blue whisper of it cool
against my cheek.

Other times – the school-test times,
and Dad-gets-home-too-late
to-say-goodnight times –
I wrap the arms of the dress around me,
breathing in a smell, faint as dried flowers.

I remember how she twirled around
– like a swirl of sky.

When I am old enough I will wear it.
Pulling up the white zip,
I'll laugh and spin,
calling out to my daughter:
How do I look?

Mandy Coe

PIANO LESSON

The streetlight on our corner
is the beacon I use to steer my course
to number eighty-one and Mrs Drucker.
I jump to touch the trees, their leaves
dark and sticky in the chemical light.
I watch how it stains my skin,
stick out my tongue to taste it like orange squash.
It's the colour of music –
not Mrs Drucker's music, not *The Fairy Waltz*,
but something wild with drums.
The thought of half an hour at the piano
stretches like my shadow
as I reach the mid-point between this lamp and the next.
I fizz like a wasp trapped under a glass,
blurting excuses why I haven't practised.

Jean Sprackland

THERE WAS NO TELLING

There was no telling what it was.
Some thought it large, some thought it small,
Some called it round, though some said square –
Some swore it had no shape at all!

The same with temperature and colour.
This one said hot, that one said cold;
One called it purple, but another
Green – and a third said gold.

Its smell, they variously claimed,
Was sweet as woodbine, sour as sweat;
Its taste pure peppermint or parsnip
Or cyanide or vinaigrette.

They disagreed about its weight,
Its height, depth, length, until their jaws
Ached contradicting one another.
There was no telling what it was.

The truth is, each one took his rod,
Swearing the rest were deaf, dumb, blind,
And sloped off to a place apart:
Each fished the pool of his own dark mind.

Raymond Wilson

18

SHUT DOWN

You watch your shoes step and scuff. Your heavy
school-bag swings around. Worry-words rattle
against your teeth. You've seen enough
and you've shut down.

You've lost your senses one by one; a sleepwalker
barely feeling the ground. Too many raised voices,
slamming doors. You've heard enough
and you've shut down.

Above you, a cloud forms the shape of your face,
a twist of wind makes it frown. A shaft of sunlight
strokes your hair, but you've felt enough
and you've shut down.

'Look up here,' whispers the tree. A single blackbird
calls your name. The promise of rain is sweet
on your tongue. But you've had enough
and you've shut down.

Mandy Coe

FIRST DOG ON THE MOON

'Hi there,
First Dog on the Moon,
How do you feel?'

Like nothing on Earth.

'Yes, but can you taste anything up there?'

Bones so cold and dry
They bite my tongue.

'That's great, First Dog on the Moon.
Now what can you smell?'

Fear of the things hiding in
hard shadows.

'OK, OK, so what can you see?'

Long dead forests,
Broken winds in empty streets,
Things,
Shadows.

'So what are you going to do next,
First Dog on the Moon?'

Sit and howl at the Earth.

David Orme

SAM'S SONG

My favourite walk
is across the fields –
we leave behind the stupid sheep
with their wonderful stink
and their *bleat, bleat, bleat*
then my human stops
and unfastens my lead . . .

I race to the river, shallow
and clear, stony and wide
and I take a run
as it's surely alive!

I stand on the stones,
snap at the water
trying to catch it
but just as I've caught
a great bite of it – *Woof!*
and I'm barking . . .

Woof! Woof! I go, barking
Woof! Woof! in the water
(occasional *Snap!* at it)
Woof! I go
   heartily
         loving
        the barking . . .
my whole body thrills to it.

Somewhere a faint calling –
my human is yelling
but all I know *Woof! Woof!* is water
and *Woof! Woof!*
I'm *Woof! Woof! Woof!*
   loving it
     loving this
Woof! Woof! Woof!
   barking.

Joan Poulson

FIVE HAIKU FOR FIVE SENSES

Grey-pink in the dawn
sitting like far distant cloud:
a new mountain range.

From a long distance
even my father's cooking
smells a bit like food

After the dentist's
I spoon soup into my mouth –
or mostly my mouth.

'Easy listening'
my father calls his music.
We all disagree.

Panting on my bike
the autumn rain in my mouth
tastes of the winter.

David Bateman

UNEXPLAINED THINGS ABOUT MY DAD

Inside his favourite hat
there's strange piano music:
Listen.

At the back of his head
there's a tattoo of a polar bear riding a bike:
Look.

If you get very close to his thumb
there's the scent of a tropical storm:
Smell.

Run your hands over his left ear
and you feel the outline of a tree:
Touch.

If he gives you a mint
it has the same flavour as pencil shavings:
Taste.

Ian McMillan

THE WAY BACK

Silence and nothing else brings you awake
In the night and you don't know where you are.
Go to the window, now, stare out at the dark,
How can you tell if it's near or far –
The light of a star in the lap of the lake?

How often have you looked at this photograph,
Edge with the glare of the morning sun?
A lake surrounded by firs . . . Remember your laugh
Ringing the shoreline? Remember you won
In the echo competition? Remember how
Night was a long time coming, how you could row
Gently across, oars dipping light as a leaf?

Sometimes your shout would return to tease,
Mixed up with another voice. HELLO—Hello . . .
Everyone wanted to try their special bellow
Like children lost in the woods. A mellow,
Lemony-scent came to you on the breeze.

The way back was through the pines
Or sometimes across the orchard, a short walk
Under a flawless sky. The fruit would fall
Cleanly into our hands, fresh from the stalk,
Hard and warm. We stuffed our pockets full.

To go there again, imagine the sky growing dark
And the evening star hanging low across the lake.
Stand by the window: away to the east
The tips of the pines are dissolving in mist.
Everything just as it was. Of lemons, only the aftertaste.

David Harsent

HIDE AND SEEK

Call out. Call loud: 'I'm ready! Come and find me!'
The sacks in the toolshed smell like the seaside.
They'll never find me in this salty dark,
But be careful that your feet aren't sticking out.
Wiser not to risk another shout.
The floor is cold. They'll probably be searching
The bushes near the swing. Whatever happens
You mustn't sneeze when they come prowling in.
And here they are, whispering at the door;
You've never heard them sound so hushed before.
Don't breathe. Don't move. Stay dumb. Hide in your blindness.
They're moving closer, someone stumbles, mutters;
Their words and laughter scuffle and they're gone.
But don't come out just yet; they'll try the lane,
And then the greenhouse and back here again.
They must be thinking that you're very clever,
Getting more puzzled as they search all over.
It seems a long time since they went away.
Your legs are stiff, the cold bites through your coat;
The dark damp smell of sand moves in your throat.
It's time to let them know that you're the winner.
Push off the sacks. Uncurl and stretch. That's better!
Out of the shed and call to them 'I've won!'
'Here I am! Come and own up I've caught you!'
The darkening garden watches. Nothing stirs.
The bushes holding their breath; the sun is gone.
Yes, here you are. But where are they who sought you?

Vernon Scannell

28

THE PUDDLE

A boy in a yellow sweater
kicks up the waste ground
between broken-glass building
and broken-glass wall.
A claw of wind tugs at the skin
of a grey puddle. He watches
the milk float glide past, quiet and shiny.
He longs to jump aboard
and break bottles.

The sun comes out
and the puddle clears.
Clouds race across its sparkling surface.
Everything changes. The boy dreams
meadows and waterfalls, forests and cliffs.
He can smell grass and taste salt,
hear seagulls shrieking
and water shuffling stones.
The world opens out for a moment:
blue and white and empty and full of itself.

Jean Sprackland

A SENSE-LESS POEM

I'm having trouble with my ears—
they do not see so well.
My eyes are also failing fast—
they've lost their sense of smell.
My nose has lost its power of speech,
my tongue, its sense of touch;
alas, your sympathy's in vain—
my hands can't hear you much.

Carey Blyton

MY UNCOMMON SENSES

I touch the taste
And I taste the sound.
Today my senses are
The wrong way round.

I can see the smell
I can hear the view.
Today my senses
Are all askew.

So I hear how you feel
And I smell what you say.
My senses are really
Quite strange today.

David Bateman

GOODNIGHT, STEPHEN

At first it was the smell,
the smell of a torch
drifting up like mist through the field.

Then it was the sound,
the sound of a torch,
a noise like a torchbeam unzipping the tent.

Now it's the weight
the weight of a torchbeam
across the sleeping bag on to my face.

I must be asleep
but I think I'm waking up.

The stink of the torchbeam
smells awful, smells scary.
A torchbeam feels spiky.

The taste of the torchbeam
tastes rotten, tastes fishy.
A torchbeam feels chilly.

I think I'm waking up.
I can't be asleep.

Then it was the smell,
the smell of a pipe
through the flap of the tent,

and it was the sound,
the sound of my dad
saying, 'Just checking. Goodnight.'

Now it's the weight, the weight of my head
on the pillow as darkness returns.

Ian McMillan

SENSATIONAL TRIALS

The smell
Of the perfume thief
Who reeked havoc in court
Then claimed he was in a scent.

The sound
Of the racket-ear
Who plugged his two lugholes
And said he'd deafened himself.

The sight
Of the pub robber
Who stole the optics
And a pair of glasses.
His trial became a spectacle case.

The taste
Of the unsavoury character
Up for a salt
Who added spice to the affair
By trying to curry flavour with the jury.

The touch
Of what felt like rough justice
When, at a stroke, hard labour
Brought them all to their senses.

Nick Toczek

THANKSGIVING

Thank You
 for all my hands can hold –
  apples red,
   and melons gold,
    yellow corn
     both ripe and sweet,
      peas and beans
       so good to eat!

Thank You
 for all my eyes can see –
  lovely sunlight,
   field and tree,
    white cloud-boats
     in sea-deep sky,
      soaring bird
       and butterfly.

Thank You
 for all my ears can hear –
  birds' song echoing
   far and near,
    songs of little
     stream, big sea,
      cricket, bullfrog,
       duck and bee!

Ivy O. Eastwick

PRAYER FOR EARTH

Last night
an owl
called from the hill.
Coyotes howled.
A deer stood still
nibbling at bushes far away.
The moon shone silver.
Let this stay.

Today
two noisy crows
flew by,
their shadows pasted to the sky.
The sun broke out
through clouds of grey.
An iris opened.
Let this stay.

Myra Cohn Livingston

SIGHT

SPECIAL TELESCOPE

I invented a special telescope
that could gently bend light
and make the air seem so clear
it could see right round the world.

I took my telescope
to the top of the nearest mountain
to try it out.

Beyond the mountains
I saw rivers, oceans, distant lands
with cities and towns,
then another ocean
and beyond it, in the far, far distance,
another mountain.

On top of the mountain,
tiny but clear, stood a man
with his back to me.

David Bateman

ACCOUNTABILITY

The musician Bruckner was handicapped
by a counting obsession which overcame
him when he was tired.

Life is wearing me down
by a process of attrition, multiplication
and unnecessary movement –
largely on the part of birds.

The number of windows in the street
is easily achievable: furrows in a field,
berries on a branch. The thirty-seven roses
on my counterpane are unequivocal.

But the swallows make my heart race
with their terrible interweaving:
and what I dread is a clear sky
at night. Always at dusk,
I am drawn to the window. Reluctantly
I turn my face upwards.

Connie Bensley

I ASKED THE LITTLE BOY WHO CANNOT SEE

I asked the little boy who cannot see,
'And what is colour like?'
'Why, green,' said he,
'Is like the rustle when the wind blows through
The forest; running water, that is blue;
And red is like a trumpet sound; and pink
Is like the smell of roses; and I think
That purple must be like a thunderstorm;
And yellow is like something soft and warm;
And white is a pleasant stillness when you lie
And dream.'

Anon.

BLIND HORSE

He snuffles towards
pouches of water in the grass
and doesn't drink
when he finds them.

He twitches listlessly
at sappy grass stems and stands
stone still, his hanging head
caricatured with a scribble
of green whiskers.

Sometimes that head swings high,
ears cock – and he stares
down a long sound,
he stares and whinnies
for what never comes.

His eyes never close
not in the heat of the day
when his leather lip droops and
he wears blinkers of flies.

At any time of the night
you hear him in his dark field
stamp the ground, stamp
the world down, waiting impatiently
for the light to break.

Norman MacCaig

THE DUNCE

He says no with his head
but he says yes with his heart
he says yes to what he loves
he says no to the teacher
he stands
he is questioned
and all the problems are posed
sudden laughter seizes him
and he erases all
the words and figures
names and dates
sentences and snares
and despite the teacher's threats
to the jeers of infant prodigies
with chalk of every colour
on the blackboard of misfortune
he draws the face of happiness.

Jacques Prevert

UNCLE EDWARD'S AFFLICTION

Uncle Edward was colour-blind;
We grew accustomed to the fact.
When he asked someone to hand him
The green book from the window-seat
And we observed its bright red cover
Either apathy or tact
Stifled comment. We passed it over.
Much later, I began to wonder
What a curious world he wandered in,
Down streets where pea-green pillar boxes
Grinned at a fire engine as green;
How Uncle Edward's sky at dawn
And sunset flooded marshy green.
Did he ken John Peel with his coat so green
And Robin Hood in Lincoln red?
On country walks avoid being stung
By nettles hot as a witch's tongue?

What meals he savoured with his eyes:
Green strawberries and fresh red peas,
Green beef and greener burgundy.
All unscientific, so it seems:
His world was not at all like that,
So those who claim to know have said.
Yet, I believe, in war-smashed France
He must have crawled from neutral mud
To lie in pastures dark and red
And seen, appalled, on every blade
The rain of innocent green blood.

Vernon Scannell

JUST CLOSE YOUR EYES

In a minute
in my head
an empty box
  a haircut
    my friend's breath
      a teacher's voice
        a blackbird singing
          what did I do on Saturday?
          What shall I do at three?
          A shiny floor
          a squeaking chair
          what does a poet eat for tea?
          has a minute gone?
        what can I write?
      who's watching me?
this minute
    in my head.

Judith Nicholls

WHO HAS SEEN THE WIND?

Who has seen the wind?
  Neither I nor you:
But when the leaves hang trembling
  The wind is passing thro'.

Who has seen the wind?
  Neither you nor I:
But when the trees bow down their heads
  The wind is passing by.

Christina Rossetti

THE BLIND MEN AND THE ELEPHANT

It was six men of Indostan
  To learning much inclined,
Who went to see the Elephant
  (Though all of them were blind),
That each by observation
  Might satisfy his mind.

The First approached the Elephant,
  And happening to fall
Against his broad and sturdy side,
At once began to bawl:
'God bless me! but the Elephant
  Is very like a wall!'

The Second, feeling of the tusk,
  Cried, 'Ho! what have we here
So very round and smooth and sharp?
  To me 'tis mighty clear
This wonder of an Elephant
  Is very like a spear!'

The Third approached the animal,
  And happening to take
The squirming trunk within his hands,
Thus boldly up and spake:
'I see,' quoth he, 'the Elephant
  Is very like a snake!'

The Fourth reached out an eager hand,
    And felt about the knee.
'What most this wondrous beast is like
    Is mighty plain,' quoth he;
'Tis clear enough the Elephant
    Is very like a tree!'

The Fifth who chanced to touch the ear,
  - Said: 'E'en that blindest man
Can tell what this resembles most;
    Deny the fact you can,
This marvel of an Elephant
    Is very like a fan!'

The Sixth no sooner had begun
    About the beast to grope,
Than, seizing on the swinging tail
    That fell within his scope,
'I see,' quoth he, 'the Elephant
    Is very like a rope!'

And so these men of Indostan
    Disputed loud and long,
Each in his own opinion
    Exceeding stiff and strong,
Though each was partly in the right,
    And all were in the wrong!

                    John Godfrey Saxe

ORANGES

The first time I walked
With a girl, I was twelve,
Cold, and weighted down
With two oranges in my jacket.
December. Frost cracking
Beneath my steps, my breath
Before me, then gone,
As I walked towards
Her house, the one whose
Porch light burned yellow
Night and day, in any weather.
A dog barked at me, until
She came out pulling
At her gloves, face bright
With rouge. I smiled,
Touched her shoulder, and led
Her down the street, across
A used car lot and a line
Of newly planted trees,
Until we were breathing
Before a drugstore. We
Entered, the tiny bell
Bringing a saleslady
Down a narrow aisle of goods.
I turned to the candies
Tiered like bleachers,
And asked what she wanted –
Light in her eyes, smiled
Started at the corners

Of her mouth. I fingered
A nickel in my pocket,
And when she lifted a chocolate
That cost a dime,
I didn't say anything.
I took the nickel from
My pocket, then an orange,
And set them quietly on
The counter. When I looked up,
The Lady's eyes met mine,
And held them, knowing
Very well what it was all
About.

Outside
A few cars hissing past,
Fog hanging like old
Coats between the trees.
I took my girl's hand
In mine for two blocks,
Then released it to let
Her unwrap the chocolate.
I peeled my orange
That was so bright against
The grey of December
That, from some distance,
Someone might have thought
I was making a fire in my hands.

Gary Soto

A BOWL OF FRUIT

In the wooden bowl
(wood coloured) are 4 apples,
3 pears and an orange.
Can you see them?

What colour are the pears?
Green? Correct. (Although
they might have been yellow.)

The apples? Wrong.
3 green and one red.

The orange? Of course,
orange. Secure in the sense
of its own glowing identity
the Lord of the Bowl
reigns over the room.
Cezanne of citrus.
Plump Picasso of peel.

Roger McGough

UNCLE AND AUNTIE

my auntie gives me a colouring book and crayons
I begin to colour
after a while auntie leans over and says
you've gone over the lines
what do you think they're there for
eh?
some kind of statement is it?
going to be a rebel are we?
your auntie gives you a lovely present
and you have to go and ruin it
I begin to cry
my uncle gives me a hanky and some blank paper
do some doggies of your own he says
I begin to colour
when I have done
he looks over
and says they are all very good
he is lying
only some of them are

John Hegley

THE COLOUR OF MY DREAMS

I'm a really rotten reader
the worst in all the class,
the sort of rotten reader
that makes you want to laugh.

I'm last in all the readin' tests,
my score's not on the page
and when I read to teacher
she gets in such a rage.

She says I cannot form my words
she says I can't build up
and that I don't know phonics
– and don't know c-a-t from k-u-p.

They say that I'm dyslexic
(that's a word they've just found out)
 . . . but when I get some plasticine
I know what that's about.

I make these scary monsters
I draw these secret lands
and get my hair all sticky
and paint on all me hands.

I make these super models,
I build these smashing towers
that reach up to the ceiling
– and take me hours and hours.

I paint these lovely pictures
in thick green drippy paint
that gets all on the carpet –
and makes the cleaners faint.

I build great magic forests
weave bushes out of string
and paint pink panderellos
and birds that really sing.

I play my world of real believe
I play it every day
and teachers stand and watch me
but don't know what to say.

They give me diagnostic tests,
they try out reading schemes,
but none of them will ever know
the colour of my dreams.

Peter Dixon

PAINT BOX

He tried to tell them what he felt,
could say it only in colours –
Sunday's white page shading to grey
of evening clocks and bells-in-the-rain.
Monday morning, bright yellow brass
of a cock crowing.
Story-time, purple.
Scarlet is shouting in the playground.

His world's a cocoon
round as an egg, an acorn
sprouting green.
The schoolroom square and hard,
his desk hard and square
facing the enemy blackboard.

'You must learn to read,' they said
and gave him a painting-book alphabet.
Apple swelled beautifully red. Balloon
expanded in blue.
C was a cage for a bird;
his brush wavered through
painting himself
a small brown smudge inside.

Phoebe Hesketh

LOST RAINBOW

One day
coming home from school
(where else?)
I found a rainbow
Lost
and sad
and torn
and broken
on a garage forecourt.
I picked it up,
wrapped it in a Wonderloaf wrapper
(which was also lost)
and took it home
where I warmed it
and dried it
in front of my mother's fire
But it died.

I think it must have been
a very old rainbow.

Peter Dixon

MY HEART LEAPS UP WHEN I BEHOLD

My heart leaps up when I behold
  A rainbow in the sky;
So was it when my life began;
So is it now I am a man;
So be it when I shall grow old.
  Or let me die!
The Child is father of the Man;
And I could wish my days to be
Bound each to each by natural piety.

William Wordsworth

AUTUMN FIRES

In the other gardens
  And all up the vale,
From the autumn bonfires
  See the smoke trail!

Pleasant summer over
  And all the summer flowers,
The red fire blazes,
  The grey smoke towers.

Sing a song of seasons!
  Something bright in all!
Flowers in the summer,
  Fires in the fall!

R. L. Stevenson

CRAB APPLE JELLY

Every year you said it wasn't worth the trouble –
you'd better things to do with your time –
and it made you furious when the jars
were sold at the church fête
for less than the cost of the sugar.

And every year you drove into the lanes
around Calverton to search
for the wild trees whose apples
looked as red and as sweet as cherries,
and tasted sourer than gooseberries.

You cooked them in the wide copper pan
Grandma brought with her from Wigan,
smashing them against the sides
with a long wooden spoon to split
the skins, straining the pulp

through as an old muslin nappy.
It hung for days, tied with string
to the kitchen steps, dripping
into a bowl on the floor –
brown-stained, horrible,

a head in a bag, a pouch
of sourness, of all that went wrong
in that house of women. The last drops
you wrung out with your hands;
then, closing doors and windows
to shut out the clamouring wasps,
you boiled up the juice with sugar,
dribbling the syrup on to a cold plate
until it set to a glaze,
filling with heated jars.

When the jars were cool
you held one up to the light
to see if the jelly had cleared.
Oh Mummy, it was as clear and shining
as stained glass and the colour of fire.

Vicki Feaver

ECLIPSE

I looked the sun straight in the eye.
He put on dark glasses.

F. R. Scott

WHAT IS . . . THE SUN?

The sun is an orange dinghy
    sailing across a calm sea

It is a gold coin
    dropped down a drain in heaven.

It is a yellow beach ball
    kicked high into the summer sky.

It is a red thumb print
    on a sheet of pale blue paper.

It is the gold top from a milk bottle
    floating on a puddle.

Wes Magee

THE RED WHEELBARROW

so much depends
upon

a red wheel
barrow

glazed with rain
water

beside the white
chickens

William Carlos Williams

A POOL AT NIGHT

Quiet,
    Stillness,
        The cool night air shimmers;
Silence.
      Frog:
And the moon disappears in widening circles.

Steven Cosmann

COLOUR

Wear it
Like a banner
For the proud –
Not like a shroud.
Wear it
Like a song
Soaring high –
Not moan or cry.

Langston Hughes

WHAT IS PINK?

What is pink? a rose is pink
By the fountain's brink.
What is red? a poppy's red
In its barley bed.
What is blue? the sky is blue
Where the clouds float thro'
What is white? a swan is white
Sailing in the light.
What is yellow? pears are yellow,
Rich and ripe and mellow.
What is green? the grass is green,
With small flowers between.
What is violet? clouds are violet
In the summer twilight.
What is orange? why, an orange,
Just an orange!

Christina Rossetti

THE SECRET SONG

Who saw the petals
   drop from the rose?
I, said the spider,
But nobody knows.

Who saw the sunset
   flash on a bird?
I, said the fish,
But nobody heard.

Who saw the fog
   come over the sea?
I, said the sea pigeon,
Only me.

Who saw the first
   green light of the sun?
I, said the night owl,
The only one.

Who saw the moss
   creep over the stone?
I, said the grey fox,
All alone.

Margaret Wise Brown

BLUE WISH

When the gas-fire glows
   It tingles with a
      Low
       Blue light.
       It

Dances with a slow
   Flicker of wishing:
Wish I may,
   Wish I might

Have a blue wish
   Always burning,
Noon,
   Burning,
      Night.

Kit Wright

THE BLUE ROOM

My room is blue, the carpet's blue
The chairs are blue, the door's blue too.
A blue bird flew in yesterday,
I don't know if it's flown away.

Richard Edwards

PIED BEAUTY

Glory be to God for dappled things –
    For skies of couple-colour as a brinded cow;
      For rose-moles all in stipple upon trout that swim;
Fresh-firecoal chestnut-falls; finches' wings;
    Landscape plotted and pieced – fold, fallow, and plough;
      And all trades, their gear and tackle and trim.

All things counter, original, spare, strange;
    Whatever is fickle, freckled (who knows how?)
      With swift, slow; sweet, sour; adazzle, dim;
He fathers-forth whose beauty is past change:
        Praise him.

Gerard Manley Hopkins

SEEING THINGS

Suddenly, the pool is alive
with small boys; they weave
and wriggle, slippery as tadpoles,
until they are summoned to order
down at the shallow end.

I make a decorous turn
in the deeper water,
and something catches my eye
far below. A childlike figure
is spread-eagled at the bottom of the pool
I try to scream, but water
fills my mouth:

The figure drifts, in slow motion,
towards the side – I follow
dumb with fear, heart knocking,
ready to grasp at hair, at limbs:

it blooms upwards, growing like magic
and comes out of the water
as a burly, bearded man,
who heaves himself up the steps,
checks his watch, and turns,
placidly, towards the high board.

Connie Bensley

THERE'S NO NEED TO LIGHT A NIGHT LIGHT

There's no need to light a night light
On a light night like tonight;
For a night light's just a slight light
On a light night like tonight.

Anon.

SOUND

SOUNDS LIKE MAGIC

I listened to a seashell
and thought I could hear
the rushing of the waves
inside my ear.

I held an empty eggshell
close against my head
and thought I heard a pecking chick
hatching from its bed.

I found a hollow coconut
and listened for a sound
and thought I heard horses' hooves
pounding on the ground.

I took an empty teacup
to see what I might hear
and thought I heard a giant's voice
booming in my ear.

Celia Warren

SNOWY MORNING

Wake
gently this morning
to a different day.
Listen.

There is no bray
of buses,
no brake growls,
no siren howls and
no horns
blow.
There is only
the silence
of a city
hushed
by snow.

Lilian Moore

QUIETER THAN SNOW

I went to school a day too soon
And couldn't understand
Why silence hung in the yard like sheets
Nothing to flap or spin, no creaks
Or shocks of voices, only air.

And the car park empty of teachers' cars
Only the first September leaves
Dropping like paper. No racks of bikes
No kicking legs, no fights,
No voices, laughter, anything . . .

Berlie Doherty

LIGHTING A FIRE

One quick scratch
Of a kitchen match
And giant flames unzip!

How do they store
So huge a roar
In such a tiny tip?

X. J. Kennedy

EARS

Have you thought to give three cheers
For the usefulness of ears?
Ears will often spring surprises
Coming in such different sizes.
Ears are crinkled, even folded.
Ears turn pink when you are scolded.
Ears can have the oddest habits
Standing rather straight on rabbits.
Ears are little tape recorders
Catching all the family orders.
Words, according to your mother,
Go in one and out the other.
Each side of your head you'll find them.
Don't forget to wash behind them.
Precious little thanks they'll earn you
Hearing things that don't concern you.

Max Fatchen

NO-SPEAKS

I am the child who stopped talking
Three years ago. There was heavy snow.
It was a blow to my family, I know.
They call me No-Speaks.
It has been one hundred and fifty-six weeks
Since I came to the decision about speech.
I clocked it was a waste of time,
to talk in plain speech or rhyme.
So, I watch the telling hands chime.
I watch the trees grow big beards, fuzzy hair.
Then, I watch them get alopecia.
I watch the snow melt into summer.
I hold my tongue round the clock.
They call me No-Speaks.
I shut my mouth from season to season.
I have a very good reason
For never saying a single world.
Not a single dickie bird.
(I was not struck by lightning.
I did not witness something shocking.)
(If two people tell the same lie
at the same time, one will die
Before the year is over.)
My lips are sealed, January to December.
They call me No-Speaks.
I am a closed book. A sealed letter.
A shut letterbox.
I despise the blether, the chatterbox.

Since I shut my trap,
Life is much better.
But every sound is an electric shock.
Leaves are shy when they first
fall from trees.

Jackie Kay

LOUDER!

OK, Andrew, nice and clearly – off you go.

Welcome everybody to our school concert . . .

Louder, please, Andrew. Mums and dads won't hear you at
the back, will they?

Welcome everybody to our school concert.

Louder, Andrew. You're not trying.
Pro – ject – your – voice.
Take a b i g b r e a t h and louder!

Welcome everybody to our school concert . . .

For goodness sake, Andrew. LOUDER! LOUDER!

Welcome every body to our school concert!

Now, Andrew, there's no need to be silly.

Roger Stevens

SILENCIO

silencio   silencio   silencio
silencio   silencio   silencio
silencio   silencio
silencio   silencio   silencio
silencio   silencio   silencio

Eugen Gomringer

HAIKU

On the temple bell
Settles – and is sleeping –
A butterfly.

Buson

ONLY

Only a tap drip, dripping
In the courtyard, by the wall
Where cushiony mosses flourish
And fleshy ferns grow tall.
Only a shutter rattling
When the wind decides to call,
Only a creeping of shadows
As night begins to fall.
Only a whisper of memories
In the lonely air of the hall.

John Cotton

The neighbours' dog will not stop barking.
He is barking the same high, rhythmic bark
that he barks every time they leave the house.
They must switch him on on their way out.

The neighbours' dog will not stop barking.
I close all the windows in the house
and put on a Beethoven symphony full blast
but I can still hear him muffled under the music,
barking, barking, barking,

and now I can see him sitting in the orchestra,
his head raised confidently as if Beethoven
had included a part for barking dog.

When the record finally ends he is still barking,
sitting there in the oboe section barking,
his eyes fixed on the conductor who is
entreating him with his baton

while the other musicians listen in respectful
silence to the famous barking dog solo,
that endless coda that first established
Beethoven as an innovative genius.

Billy Collins

NOVEMBER NIGHT

Listen . . .
With faint dry sound,
Like steps of passing ghosts,
The leaves, frost-crisped, break from the trees
And fall.

Adelaide Crapsey

THE CELLO

To tell you
the truth
I never
wanted to be
a cello.
When I was
wood
I had
my own song.

Lorena Bruff

MUSIC

Let me go where'er I will
I hear a sky-born music still:
It sounds from all things old,
It sounds from all things young;
From all that's fair, from all that's foul,
Peals out a cheerful song.

It is not only in the rose,
It is not only in the bird,
Not only where the rainbow glows,
Nor in the song of woman heard,
But in the darkest, meanest things

There always, always something sings.
'Tis not in the high stars alone,
Nor in the cups of budding flowers,
Nor in the redbreast's mellow tone,
Nor in the bow that smiles in showers,
But in the mud and scum of things
There always, always something sings.

Ralph Waldo Emerson

THE NOISE THAT TIME MAKES

The noise that Time makes in passing by
Is very slight but even you can hear it,
Having not necessarily to be near it,
Needing only the slightest will to try:
Hold the receiver of a telephone
To your ear when no one is talking on the line
And what may at first sound to you like the whine
Of wind over distant wires is Time's own
Garments brushing against a windy cloud.
That same noise again but not so well
May be heard by taking a small cockle-shell
From the sand and holding it against your head;
Then you can hear Time's footsteps as they pass
Over the earth brushing the eternal grass.

Merrill Moore

JOY AT THE SOUND

Joy at the silver birch in the morning sunshine
Joy at the spring-green of its fingertips

Joy at the swirl of cold milk in the blue bowl
Joy at the blink of its bubbles

Joy at the cat revving up on the lawn
Joy at the frogs that leapfrog to freedom

Joy at the screen as it fizzes to life
Joy at The Simpsons, Lisa and Bart

Joy at the dentist: 'Fine, see you next year'
Joy at the school gates: 'Closed'.

Joy at the silver withholding the chocolate
Joy at the poem, two verses to go

Joy at the zing of the strings of the racquet
Joy at the bounce of the bright yellow ball

Joy at the key unlocking the door
Joy at the sound of her voice in the hall

Roger McGough

ANIMALS WITH LONG EARS

Animals with long ears
    Can hear every little sound:
A butterfly on tiptoe
    Snow settling on the ground

A rose blinking in the sunlight
    The last breath of a bee
The heartbeat of an egg
    Leaves taking leave of the tree

The shimmy of a golden carp
    The hiatus of a hawk
The wriggle of a baited worm
    The bobbing of a cork

The echo in a coral reef
   The moon urging the tide
A cloud changing shape
   They listen, open-eyed.

Animals with long ears
   Hear such sounds every day
and try to recapture
   In a melodious way

The music that surrounds them
   So isn't it sad to say
That being tone-deaf their chorus
   Is an ear-crunching BRAY.

Roger McGough

BEFORE THE DAYS OF NOAH

Before the days of Noah
before he built his ark
seagulls sang like nightingales
and lions sang like larks.
The tortoise had a mighty roar
the cockerel had a moo
kitten always eeyored
and elephants just mewed.
It was the way the world was
 . . . when owls had a bark
and dogs did awful crowings
whilst running round the park.
Horses baaaed like baa lambs
ducks could all miaow
and animals had voices
quite different from now!
But, came the day of flooding
and all the world was dark
the animals got weary
of living in the ark –
So they swapped around their voices
a trumpet for a mew
– a silly sort of pastime
when nothing much to do.

But when the flood had ended
and the world was nice and dry
the creatures had forgotten
how once they hissed or cried.

So they kept their brand-new voices
– forgot the days before
– when lions used to giggle
and gerbils used to roar.

Peter Dixon

PLEASANT SOUNDS

The rustling of leaves under the feet in woods and under
  hedges;
The crumping of cat-ice and snow down wood-rides,
  narrow lanes, and every street causeway;
Rustling through a wood or rather rushing, while the wind
  halloos in the oak-top like thunder;
The rustle of birds' wings startled from their nests or flying
  unseen into the bushes;
The whizzing of larger birds overhead in a wood, such as
  crows, puddocks, buzzards;
The trample of robins and wood-larks on the brown leaves,
  and the patter of squirrels on the green moss;
The fall of an acorn on the ground, the pattering of nuts
  on the hazel branches as they fall from ripeness;
The flirt of the ground lark's wing from the stubbles –
  how sweet such pictures on dewy mornings, when the
dew flashes from its brown feathers!

John Clare

EARS HEAR

Flies buzz,
Motors roar.
Kettles hiss,
People snore.
Dogs bark,
Birds cheep.
Autos honk: *Beep! Beep!*

Winds sigh,
Shoes squeak.
Trucks honk,
Floors creak.
Whistles toot,
Bells clang,
Doors slam: *Bang! Bang!*

Kids shout,
Clocks ding.
Babies cry,
Phones ring.
Balls bounce,
Spoons drop.
People scream: *Stop! Stop!*

Lucia M. and James L. Humes Jr.

OF NOTHING AT ALL: ORDERS

Muffle the wind;
Silence the clock;
Muzzle the mice;
Curb the small talk;
Cure the hinge-squeak;
Banish the thunder.
Let me sit silent,
Let me wonder.

A. M. Klein

SOMETIMES

Sometimes
when I skip or hop
or when I'm
      jumping

Suddenly
I like to stop
and listen to me
      thumping.

Lilian Moore

NOISE

I like noise.
The whoop of a boy, the thud of a hoof,
The rattle of rain on a galvanised roof,
The hubbub of traffic, the roar of a train,
The throb of machinery numbing the brain,
The switching of wires of an overhead tram,
The rush of the wind, a door on the slam,
The boom of the thunder, the crash of the waves,
The din of a river that races and raves,
The crack of a rifle, the clank of a pail,
The strident tattoo of a swift-slapping sail –
From any old sound that the silence destroys,
Arises a gamut of soul-stirring joys.
I like noise.

Jessie Pope

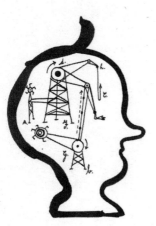

BABBLING AND GABBLING

My Granny's an absolute corker,
My Granny's an absolute cracker,
But she's Britain's speediest talker
And champion yackety-yacker!

Everyone's fond of my Granny,
Everyone thinks she's nice,
But before you can say Jack Robinson,
My Granny's said it twice!

Kit Wright

PEOPLE

Some people talk and talk
and never say a thing.
Some people look at you
and birds begin to sing.

Some people laugh and laugh
and yet you want to cry.
Some people touch your hand
and music fills the sky.

Charlotte Zolotow

LOUDER THAN A CLAP OF THUNDER!

Louder than a clap of thunder,
louder than an eagle screams,
louder than a dragon blunders,
or a dozen football teams,
louder than a four-alarmer,
or a rushing waterfall,
louder than a knight in armour
jumping from a ten-foot wall.

Louder than an earthquake rumbles,
louder than a tidal wave,
louder than an ogre grumbles
as he stumbles through his cave,
louder than stampeding cattle
louder than a cannon roars,
louder than a giant's rattle,
that's how loud my father *SNORES!*

Jack Prelutsky

LIFE IS A BUCKET

(A noisy poem)

Put him in a cave
He'd find a door to slam

Let loose on a cloud
A can to kick

Playing in a haystack
He'd find a plate to smash

Alone on the moon
A balloon to burst

He just can't help it
He's one of those boys

Life is a bucket, so boring
When not filled with noise.

Roger McGough

MY BROTHER

My brother is loud.
His shouts bounce off the walls
like gunshots.
If he was in a strip cartoon
his words would be
in big block capitals
all the time.
He makes everybody else sound quiet.
He's the only person I know
who can speak in a
deafening whisper.

Gus Grenfell

TOUCH

PEACH

Touch it to your cheek and it's soft
as a velvet new-born mouse
who has to strive
to be alive.

Bite in. Runny
honey
blooms on your tongue –
as if you've bitten open
a whole hive.

Rose Rauter

THE APPLE'S SONG

Tap me with your finger,
rub me with your sleeve,
hold me, sniff me, peel me
curling round and round
till I burst out white and cold
from my tight red coat
and tingle in your palm
as if I'd melt and breathe
a living pomander
waiting for the minute
of joy when you lift me
to your mouth and crush me
and in taste and fragrance
I race through your head
in my dizzy dissolve.

I sit in the bowl in my cool corner and watch as you pass
smoothing your apron.
Are you thirsty yet?
My eyes are shining.

Edwin Morgan

MY HANDS

Think of all my hands can do,
pick up a pin and do up a shoe,
they can help, they can hurt too,
or paint a summer sky bright blue.

They can throw and they can catch.
They clap the team that wins the match.
If I'm rough my hands can scratch.
If I'm rude my hands can snatch.

Gently, gently they can stroke,
carefully carry a glass of Coke,
tickle my best friend for a joke,
but I won't let them nip and poke.

My hands give and my hands take.
With Gran they bake a yummy cake.
They can mend but they can break.
Think of music hands can make.

Jo Peters

PARADISE

Climbing up into my father's
barrow of cut grass
and sinking gently, all that
thick warm moisture
moulded round me, then
the mower's hum becoming louder,
nearer, stuttering to a halt
and Dad pretending not to know
I'm in there, shaking out
another load of luscious
freshness onto me and muttering
I wonder where he is?
and me about to answer
Here I am but then
deciding not to.

John Mole

NETTLES

My son aged three fell in the nettle bed.
'Bed' seemed a curious name for those green spears,
That regiment of spite behind the shed:
It was no place for rest. With sobs and tears
The boy came seeking comfort and I saw
White blisters beaded on his tender skin.
We soothed him till his pain was not so raw.
At last he offered us a watery grin,
And then I took my hook and honed the blade
And went outside and slashed in fury with it
Till not a nettle in that fierce parade
Stood upright any more. Next task: I lit
A funeral pyre to burn the fallen dead.
But in two weeks the busy sun and rain
Had called up tall recruits behind the shed:
My son would often feel sharp wounds again.

Vernon Scannell

MARK'S FINGERS

I like my fingers.
They grip a ball,
Turn a page,
Break a fall,
Help whistle
A call.
Shake hands
And shoot
Rubber bands.
When candy is offered
They take enough.
They fill my pockets
With wonderful stuff,
And they always tell me
Smooth from rough.
They follow rivers
On a map,
They double over
When I rap,
They smack together
When I clap.
They button buttons,
Tie shoelaces,
Open doors to

Brand-new places.
They shape and float
My paper ships,
Fasten paper to
Paper clips,
And carry ice cream
To my lips . . .

Mary O'Neill

PARTY

Sitting on the stairs,
you tell me that when you were five
a boy called David Bird tried to kiss you,
missed, and fell into a bed of nettles.

I want to kiss you now,
but what would I fall off,
and what would I fall into?

Too late I move, indecisively,
and fall into the nettles.

Someone takes you gently by the hand,
smoothes your hair,
leads you back into the party.

Adrian Henri

WET

Wet wet wet
the world of melting winter,
icicles weeping themselves away
on the eaves
little brown rivers streaming
down the road
nibbling
at the edges of the tired snow,
  all puddled mud
  not a dry place to put
  a booted foot,
everything
  dripping
  slipping
  gushing
  slushing
and listen to that brook
rushing
like a puppy loosed from its leash.

Lilian Moore

FORTUNE

Fortune
 has its cookies to give out
which is a good thing
 since it's been a long time since
 that summer in Brooklyn
when they closed off the street
 one hot day
 and the

FIREMEN

 turned on their hoses
 and all the kids ran out in it
 in the middle of the street
 and there were
 maybe a couple dozen of us

 out there
with the water squirting up
 to the
 sky
 and all over
 us
there were maybe only six of us
 kids altogether
 running around in our
 barefeet and birthday
 suits
 and I remember Molly but then
the firemen stopped squirting their hoses
 all of a sudden and went
 back in

their firehouse
                              and
    started playing pinochle again
              just as if nothing
                    had ever
                              happened
while I remember Molly
                         looked at me and
         ran in
because I guess really we were the only ones there.

                     Lawrence Ferlinghetti

PUDDLES

To jump into, jump over
splash round the side of,
feet wet and legs muddy
hearts light and free.
An aid to mud-pie-making,
puddle-jumping record breaking,
SPLASH, by surprise taking,
indignant old ladies and boys full of glee.
Then when we're tired we squelch our way home,
where there's scolding and bathings
then huggings and tea.
Then we're tucked up in bed
glowing toe-tips to head,
and we're glad that the day has been
happy and furious
muddy and glorious
wonderful
   (thank you God)
long
      live
          (yawn)
            PUDDLES.

Alwyn Marriage

MUD

Mud is very nice to feel
All squishy-squash between the toes!
I'd rather wade in wiggly mud
Than smell a yellow rose.
Nobody else but the rosebush knows
How nice mud feels
Between the toes.

Polly Chase Boyden

SQUISHY TOUCH

Everything King Midas touched
Turned to gold, the lucky fellow.
Every single thing I touch
Turns to raspberry Jell-O.
Today I touched the kitchen wall (squish),
I went and punched my brother Paul (splish).
I tried to fix my bike last week (sploosh),
And kissed my mother on the cheek (gloosh).
I got into my overshoes (sklush),
I tired to read the Evening News (smush),
I sat down in the easy chair (splush),
I tried to comb my wavy hair (slush).
I took a dive into the sea (glush) –
Would you like to shake hands with me (sklush)?

Shel Silverstein

TICKLISH TOM

Did you hear 'bout Ticklish Tom?
He got tickled by his mom.
Wiggled and giggled and fell on the floor,
Laughed and rolled right out the door.
All the way to school and then
He got tickled by his friends.
Laughed till he fell off his stool,
Laughed and rolled right out of school
Down the stairs and finally stopped
Till he got tickled by a cop.
And all the more he kept gigglin',
All the more the folks kept ticklin'.
He shrieked and screamed and rolled around,
Laughed his way right out of town.
Through the country down the road,
He got tickled by a toad.
Past the mountains across the plain,
Tickled by the falling rain,
Tickled by the soft brown grass,
Tickled by the clouds that passed.
Giggling, rolling on his back
He rolled on the railroad track.
Rumble, rumble, whistle, roar –
Tom ain't ticklish any more.

Shel Silverstein

THE ITCH

If your hands get wet
in the washing-up water,
if they get covered in flour,
if you get grease or oil
all over your fingers,
if they land up in the mud,
wet grit, paint, or glue . . .

have you noticed
it's just then
that you always get
a terrible itch
just inside your nose?
And you can try to
twitch your nose,
squeeze your nose,
scratch it with your arm,
scrape your nose on
your shoulder
or press it
up against the wall,
but it's no good.
You can't get rid of
the itch.

It drives you so mad
you just have to let a
finger get at it.
And before you know
you've done it.
You've wiped a load of glue,
or oil,
or cold wet pastry
all over the end of your nose.

Michael Rosen

ITCH

My sister had an itch
    I asked if it was catching
'Catch,' she said, and threw it.
    Now I'm the one who's scratching.

Roger McGough

SWIMMING POOL

Floating, floating weightless
In the nothingness of pool,
I am all wet thoughts.

Water-soaked, whirling hair
Melts into my skin.
I am bathed in blue.

Nothing beneath to feel.
Nothing but sky overhead.
I live outside myself.

Myra Cohn Livingston

RETURN

No moon
My boots crunch on the iced-over path.
The woods are still.
I have nowhere to go.

Then from a dark place
you jump out and throw yourself on my shoulders.
You've come back.

I will carry you,
strange rider.

Lou Lipsitz

WINTER MORNING

Take one starry night
without cloud blankets.
Sprinkle icing sugar all about.
Leave to set.

Frosted leaves
sugared trees
spider's web appears
marked out in silver pen.

Serve with hats and mitts on,
boots and scarves on.
Scrape silver from the car.
Outside's a big fridge.

By dinner time the sun
you left it to bake in
has licked up all the sugar.
Winter's work's undone.

Angela Topping

135

THE CAT

Conscious of being a cat
I am given to sensuality.
I like to slide my bulk
Against the nylon ankles of young ladies,
Then again I fold my fur
On silken eiderdowns
And take pleasure in simply walking,
Turn up my nose at meat,
Disdain creamless milk
And fattened by the heat of open fires
Compose myself for sleep
Within the tidy limits of myself
Even in the best company.

Gareth Owen

CLOSE-CROPPED HAIR

Close-cropped hair feels good.
It should.
It gives you street cred –
And as I've always said,
It feels like having eyebrows
All over your head.

Linda Marshall

CAT AND THE WEATHER

Cat takes a look at the weather.
Snow.
Puts a paw on the sill.
His perch is piled, is a pillow.

Shape of his pad appears.
Will it dig? No.
Not like sand.
Like his fur almost.

But licked, not liked.
Too cold.
Insects are flying, fainting down.
He'll try

to bat one against the pane.
They have no body and no buzz.
And now his feet are wet:
it's a puzzle.

Shakes each leg,
then shakes his skin
to get the white flies off.
Looks for his tail,

tells it to come on in
by the radiator.
World's turned queer
somehow. All white,

no smell. Well, here
inside it's still familiar.
He'll go to sleep until
it puts itself right.

May Swenson

GIVE YOURSELF A HUG

Give yourself a hug
when you feel unloved

Give yourself a hug
when people put on airs
to make you feel a bug

Give yourself a hug
when everyone seems to give you
a cold-shoulder shrug

Give yourself a hug –
a big big hug

And keep on singing
'Only one in a million like me
Only one in a million-billion-trillion-zillion
like me.'

Grace Nichols

S-T-R-E-T-C-H-I-N-G

Waking up
in the morning
is lovely.
Especially when you s-t-r-e-t-c-h.
You open up
your legs and arms
and stretch.
It's just lovely.
The feeling just makes
you want to do it
over and over again.
But after a while
your stretch
runs out
and it's over.

Sharon Cheeks

SOMERSAULTS

It's fun turning somersaults
and bouncing on the bed,
I walk on my hands
and I stand on my head.

I swing like a monkey
and I tumble and I shake,
I stretch and I bend,
But I never, never break.

I wiggle like a worm
and I wriggle like an eel,
I hop like a rabbit
and I flop like a seal.

I leap like a frog
and I jump like a flea,
there must be a rubber
inside of me.

Jack Prelutsky

EVERYTHING TOUCHES

Everything touches, life interweaves
Starlight and gunsmoke, ashes and leaves
Birdsong and thunder, acid and rain
Everything touches, unbroken chain.

Chainsaw and rainbow, warrior and priest
Assassin off-duty, beauty and beast
Heartbeat and high tide, ebb and flow
Cardboard cathedral covered in snow

Snowdrop and gangrene, hangman and clown
Walls that divide come tumbling down
Seen through the night the glimmer of day
Light is but darkness worn away.

Past and future, distance and time
Atom to atom, water to wine
Look all around, what do you see?
Everything touches, you're touching me

Look all around, what do you see?
Everything touches, you're touching me.

Roger McGough

SMELL

BE GLAD YOUR NOSE IS ON YOUR FACE

Be glad your nose is on your face,
not pasted on some other place,
for if it were where it is not,
you might dislike your nose a lot.

Imagine if your precious nose
were sandwiched in between your toes,
that clearly would not be a treat,
for you'd be forced to smell your feet.

Your nose would be a source of dread
were it attached atop your head,
it soon would drive you to despair,
forever tickled by your hair.

Within your ear, your nose would be
an absolute catastrophe,
for when you were obliged to sneeze,
your brain would rattle from the breeze.

Your nose, instead, through thick and thin,
remains between your eyes and chin,
not pasted on some other place –
be glad your nose is on your face!

Jack Prelutsky

NOSE TO NOSE

You looking at me? Hey, I said are you looking
At me, tough guy? OK, what's cooking –

What's that niff in the air? Could it be fear,
Or is it your dad's cologne? I hear

Behind that sneer you're not as tasty
As you like to make out; so don't be hasty,

Better keep your distance, don't say too much,
I'm no pushover, I'm no soft touch,

You can count on me to stare you down
With a glance, and run you out of town.

Think you're handy? Think you're hard?
All I see is a tub of lard.

Think you're lucky, walking tall,
Smelling of roses, on the ball,

A new kid on the block, dead cool?
Time to come to your senses, fool,

You're betting blind. Know what I feel? –
On reflection, pal, you're no big deal.

But, hey, I'm done – now it's your call
We'll see who winds up feeling small,

Let's settle things, once and for all.
Mirror, mirror, on the wall . . .

David Harsent

ODE TO MY NOSE

O Nose
Why perch upon my Face?
Could you not find
A better place?

You jut between
One Eye and tother
So neither Eye
Can see his Brother.

An easy target
For the hostile Fist.
You're an obstruction
When I want to be kissed.

And when you run
It's always South
Over my top lip
Into my Mouth.

O Nose
Why perch upon my Face?
Could you discover
No better place?

My Nose replied:
Up here I have come
As far as possible
From your Bum.

Adrian Mitchell

WOULDN'T IT BE FUNNY IF YOU DIDN'T HAVE A NOSE?

You couldn't smell your dinner
If you didn't have a nose
You couldn't tell a dirty nappy
From a summer rose
You couldn't smell the ocean
Or the traffic, I suppose
Oh wouldn't it be funny
If you didn't have a nose?

You couldn't smell your mummy
If you didn't have a nose
You couldn't tell an orange
from a row of smelly toes
You couldn't smell the burning
(Think how quick a fire grows)
Wouldn't it be funny
If you didn't have a nose?

Where would we be without our hooters?
Nothing else would really suit us.
What would we sniff through?
How would we sneeze?
What would we wipe
Upon our sleeves?

You couldn't smell a rat
If you didn't have a nose
You couldn't tell a duchess
From a herd of buffaloes
And . . . mmmm that Gorgonzola
As it starts to decompose
Oh wouldn't it be funny
If you didn't have a nose?

Where would we be without our hooters?
Nothing else would really suit us.
And think of those who
Rub their noses
Life would be tough for
Eskimoses.

You couldn't wear your glasses
If you didn't have a nose
And what would bullies aim for
When it came to blows?
Where would nostrils be without them?
When it's runny how it glows
Oh wouldn't it be funny
if you didn't have a . . .

     have a . . .

     have a . . .

       a . . .

       a . . . choo!

Roger McGough

SILLY MOO!

To warm her frozen toes
Aunt Rose chose
To stick them up her nose

Silly Moo! They stuck like glue
Until, at last, A . . .
A . . . A . . . Chooooo!

Hilary Clough

WHEN GOD GAVE OUT NOSES

When God gave out noses
I thought He said 'Roses'
So I asked for a big red one.

When He handed out legs
I thought He said 'Eggs'
So I asked for two, hard-boiled.

When He gave out looks
I thought He said 'Books'
So I said I didn't want any.

When he gave out brains
I thought He said 'Trains'
And so I missed mine.

Anon.

NOSES

I'm talking about noses
wet noses
warty noses
sleepy noses
when someone dozes

noses in hankies
noses in books
noses in crannies
noses in nooks

I'm talking about noses
noses at a flower show
the show is full of noses
noses in the tulips
noses in the roses

noses for wrinkling
noses for wiggling
noses for waggling
noses for jiggling

noses that sneeze
noses that run
noses in the wind
noses in the sun

I'm talking about noses
noses on donkeys
mice's twitching noses
the noses on the elephants
looking more like hoses

noses underwater
blowing out bubbles
noses in a fight
in all kinds of trouble

dinosaur noses
Martian nose
eyes and nose
moustache and nose

I'm talking about noses
noses on the TV
puppets' big red noses
noses on photos
noses in posies

now give those noses a wipe
give those noses a blow
pull those noses hard
and watch those noses grow.

Michael Rosen

GREEN PIECE

Show me a salad
        and I'll show you a sneeze
Anything green
        makes me weak at the knees
On St Patrick's day
        I stay home and wheeze
I have hay fever all the year round.

Broken-down lawnmowers
        Bring me out in a sweat
A still-life of flowers,
        in oils, and I get
All the sodden signs
        of a sinus upset
I have hay fever all the year round.

A chorus of birdsong
        makes my flesh creep
I dream of a picnic
        and scratch in my sleep
Counting pollen
        instead of sheep
I have hay fever all the year round.

Summertime's great
       (except for the sun)
Holly and mistletoe
       make my nose run
Autumn leaves and I swoon
       It's no fun
Having hay fever all the year round.

Roger McGough

HERE IS THE NOSE THAT
SMELLED SOMETHING SWEET

Here is the Nose that smelled something sweet
And led the search for a bite to eat

Here are the Feet that followed the Nose
Around the kitchen on ten Tiptoes

Here are the Eyes that looked high and low
till they spotted six pans sitting all in a row

Here are the Arms that reached up high
To bring down a fresh-baked blueberry pie

Here is the Mouth that opened up wide
Here are the Hands that put pie inside

Here is the Tongue that licked the tin
And lapped up the juice running down the Chin

Here is the Stomach that growled for more
Here are the Legs that ran for the door

Here are the Ears that heard a whack
Here is the Bottom that felt a smack!

Clyde Watson

MY FEET

My Feet, my feet,
I love my feet.
I think they're great,
I think they're neat.

They're pretty, pink,
and picturesque.
They look so perfect
on my desk.

Unfortunately,
sad to tell,
they also have
a funny smell.

So though I'm fast,
and though I'm fleet,
and though at sports
I can't be beat,

no team will pick
me to compete,
because they always
smell defeat.

Kenn Nesbitt

STINKERMAN

I'm Stinkerman, yes Stinkerman
stinking like a frying pan
filled with fat that's six weeks old
rancid, rotten, filled with mould
I smell of socks soaked in cheese
of rotten cabbage, putrid peas
I pong of milk that has gone sour
this is the secret of my power
you'll gag and retch, look away
and that is when I'll spoil your day.

My sweaty armpits have no hope
of ever feeling suds of soap
green fungus drips down all my teeth
my dreadful breath's beyond belief
my feet just reek, their rich aroma
certainly will knock you over
you are not even safe in bed
my awful whiff will fill your head
and as your eyes begin to close
my ghastly stench will clog your nose.

Superman fears me more
than green kryptonite
I paralyse his nerves with smells
that make him sick all night
when Batman sniffs my odours
he has to find fresh air
Spiderman just runs away
and Robin isn't there
all these superheroes
are just a foolish sham
so just remember this
I stink, therefore, I am.

David Harmer

SMELLY

Betty could smell Susan,
Susan could smell Paul,
But poor little Christopher
Couldn't smell at all.

Betty smelt of hyacinths,
Susan smelt of cats
That smelt as if they'd spent all night
Chasing one-eyed rats;
Paul smelt of bubblegum
Rolled up in a ball –
But sweet little Christopher
Didn't smell at all.

Dave Ward

SMELLY PEOPLE

Uncle Oswald smells of tobacco.
Aunt Agatha smells of rope.
Cousin Darren smells of aeroplane glue.
Cousin Tracey smells of soap.

My mum smells of garlic and cabbage.
My dad smells of cups of tea.
My baby sister smells of sick
and my brother of TCP.

Our classroom smells of stinky socks.
Our teacher smells of Old Spice.
I wonder what I smell of?
I'll just have a sniff . . .
hmmm . . . quite nice.

Roger Stevens

INSULT

A notion currently being inspected by
My brain is that
The glands beneath your skin
That produce minute particles
Designed to be carried
By tiny airborne currents
And picked up by nerves
In the mucous membrane
Covering the upper turbinal bone
And the nasal septum
Thus triggering impulses
Along olfactory nerves
Passing through minute holes
On the cribriform plate
Of the ethmoid bone
Into the olfactory bulb
In the nose
and so to the
Olfactory tract
In the brain
Are over-producing
Again

Or to put it
Another way –

I think
You stink!

Roger Stevens

MRS SKUNK WRITES A LETTER TO THE PRESS

Dear Editor

My husband and I were very upset
by a suggestion in your paper
that we skunks have bad breath.
You humans seem to forget
the dirty wind you let off
especially after you've gorged on beans.
And what about the smell of death
you bring to our rivers
from the fumes of your factories?
Humans have such short memories.
My husband and I both agreed
that your comment was most unfair.
What you humans call bad breath
We skunks call wee defensive warfare.
We're only protecting ourselves, you hear.

Yours Very Upset

Mrs Skunk

John Agard

STALE

You know how sometimes
you open your sandwich box
and it smells stale

and there are a few crumbs
and a biscuit wrapper
and a bit of a crisp

and you want to close it
although you know you should wash it
you want to close it.

Well, that's how I feel today.

Ian McMillan

THERE WAS A YOUNG CREATURE FROM SPACE

There was a young creature from space
Whose legs grew out of its face
The smell of its toes
Was so near its nose
It wore a clothes peg just in case.

Steve Turner

ROCK AOUND THE WOK

There's a frying and a frizzling
   and a simmer and a sizzling
   in the WOK . . .

There's a bunch o' crazy bean shoots
   and the shoots are pretty meanshoots
   in the WOK . . .

There's a ginger root a-jumping
   and a lotta stalks a-stumping
   in the WOK . . .

There's onions that are springing
   and there's flavours that are singing
   in the WOK . . .

So,
Baby,

LET'S GO STIR THE WOK
(oh, baby)
LET'S GO STIR THE WOK
(oh, baby)
ROCK AROUND THE WOK

Because:

There's a lotta food,
There's a lotta heat.
So shake it up!
That's enough.
Let's eat

FROM THE WOK!

Kit Wright

PRELUDES

The winter evening settles down
With smells of steaks in passageways.
Six o'clock.
The burnt-out ends of smoky days.
And now a gusty shower wraps
The grimy scraps
Of withered leaves about his feet.

And newspapers from vacant lots;
The showers beat
On broken blinds and chimney pots,
And at the corner of the street
A lonely cab-horse steams and stamps.
And then the lighting of the lamps.

T. S. Eliot

DIGGING

Today I think
Only with scents, – scents dead leaves yield,
And bracken, and wild carrot's seed,
And the square mustard field;

Odours that rise
When the spade wounds the roots of tree,
Rose, currant, raspberry, or goutweed,
Rhubarb or celery;

The smoke's smell, too,
Flowing from where a bonfire burns
The dead, the waste, the dangerous,
And all to sweetness turns.

It is enough
To smell, or crumble the dark earth,
While the robin sings over again
Sad songs of Autumn mirth.

Edward Thomas

A SOFT DAY

A soft day, thank God!
A wind from the south
With a honeyed mouth;
A scent of drenching leaves,
Briar and beech and lime,
White elderflower and thyme
And the soaking grass smells sweet,
Crushed by my two bare feet,
While the rain drips,
Drips, drips, drips from the leaves.

A soft day, thank God!
The hills wear a shroud
Of silver cloud;
The web the spider weaves
Is a glittering net;
The woodland path is wet
And the soaking earth smells sweet
Under my two bare feet,
And the rain drips,
Drips, drips, drips from the leaves.

W. M. Letts

MILLIONS OF STRAWBERRIES

Marcia and I went over the curve,
Eating our way down
Jewels of strawberries we didn't deserve,
Eating our way down
Till our hands were sticky, and our lips painted.
And over us the hot day fainted,
And we saw snakes
And got scratched
And a lust overcame us for the red unmatched
Small buds of berries,
Till we lay down –
Eating our way down –
And rolled in the berries like two little dogs,
Rolled
In the late gold.
And gnats hummed,
And it was cold,
And home we went, home without a berry,
Painted red and brown
Eating our way down.

Genevieve Taggard

AS TASTY AS A PICNIC

As salty as the sea,
As crunchy as the sand,
My banana sandwich
is curling in my hand.

As soft as the sun
As sweet as a grin,
My vanilla ice cream
is dripping down my chin.

Celia Warren

ONE MOMENT IN SUMMER

The house is dropping swallows
one by one from under the gutter

they swoop and fall
on our heads as we queue
for ice cream.

It is so hot
that the long line of cars clogging the road
hums like a line of electric fires.

They shine and shimmer, stink of oil and warm seats
the children gaze out from their misted windows.

Trapped under glass
hair plastered down with sweat
gasping for breath like frogs under ice.

The cars crawl round the curve
of the road, stuck in between the shop
and the café.

My ice cream is butterscotch and almond
Lizzie's is chocolate, Harriet's vanilla.

They are so delicious and cold
we lick them slowly, letting the long, cool flavours
slide down our tongues.

Inside the cars, the red-faced people
begin to boil.

The swallows flit and dart
rapid specks of blue, black and white
the summer flies at us
like an arrow.

David Harmer

ICE-CREAM POEM

The chiefest of young Ethel's vices
Was eating multitudes of ices.

Whene'er the ice-van's booming tinkle
Was heard, Eth ran out in a twinkle,

And gorged herself on large 'Vanilla';
Her mum foretold that it would kill 'er

No tears could thaw her; once she ran
Away and hid inside the van,

And promptly froze upon the spot
Like the salt-pillar-wife of Lot.

Poor Eth is licked! Behold the follies
Of one whose lolly went on lollies.

Though there is one thing in her favour
She now has quite a strawberry flavour.

Gerda Mayer

ADVICE TO AN ICE LOLLY LICKER

Red Rocket
on a stick.
If it shines,
lick it quick.

Clap Clap clapclapclap!

Round the edges,
on the top,
round the bottom,
do not stop.

Clap Clap clapclapclap!

Suck the Lolly.
Lick your lips.
Lick the sides
as it drips

ClapClap clapclapclap!

off the stick –
quick, quick –
lick, lick –
Red Rocket
on a stick.

Clap Clap clapclapclap!

Pie Corbett

IF YOU WERE MADE OF CHOCOLATE

If you were made of chocolate
    would you eat yourself?
Or be dressed in silver paper
    on the sweetshop shelf?

Would you have a crunchy middle
    or be filled with fudge toffee?
Would you have a special offer price
    give ten per cent more free?

Would you be long and thin and flaky
    or chunky in a bar
or sweet and sticky pieces
    filling up a jar?

If you were made of chocolate
    would you be nibbled bit by bit
Or stuffed into a mouth in one huge go?
    (Your mum would have a fit!)

If you were made of chocolate
    you'd have to mind the sun
and if your friends got hungry, well –
    it wouldn't be much fun!

If you were made of chocolate
    would you eat yourself?
Or would you sit forever
    on life's dusty sweetshop shelf?

Rupert Loydell

CHOCS

Into the half-pound box of Moonlight
my small hand crept.
There was an electrifying rustle.
There was a dark and glamorous scent.
Into my open, religious mouth
the first Marzipan Moment went.

Down in the crinkly second layer
five finger-piglets snuffled
among the Hazelnut Whirl,
the Caramel Swirl,
the Black Cherry and Almond Truffle.

Bliss.

I chomped, I gorged.
I stuffed my face,
till only the Coffee Cream
was left for the owner of the box –
tough luck, Anne Pope –
oh, and half an Orange Supreme.

Carol Ann Duffy

AT MY BIRTHDAY PARTY

At my birthday party
I had chocolate cake,
And cheesecake,
And fruitcake,
And ginger cake,
And fudge cake.
After that I had stummer cake.

Anthony Browne

MR KIPLING

When I'm feeling like a snack,
I like doughnuts and flapjack,
Angel cake or gingerbread or Bakewell tart;
But when it's time for lunch
It's Battenburg or almond crunch,
A dozen madeleines is just the start;
I'll polish off a flan
With chopped nuts and marzipan,
Then I'm on to cake, both cherry and Dundee;
I'll munch my way through oodles
Of iced buns and apple strudels,
And save the macaroons and petits fours for tea!

And it's cake, cake! cake!
There's no other food to beat it,
So let the peasants eat it,
There's nothing so delicious as a cake!

If I'm ready for a blow-out
I'll put on my coat and go out
To Tesco and inspect their stock of cake;
If I find some walnut squares,
Forest gateaux or eclairs,
Just waiting on the shelves for me to take;
If I see an almond slice,
Or Swiss roll, I'll say 'How nice',
And buy 'em with a piece of fruit Madeira,
And when my plate of cake's diminished,
I'm not sad that lunch has finished . . .
Because it means that tea is getting nearer!

And it's cake, cake! cake!
There's no other food to beat it,
So let the peasants eat it,
There's nothing so delicious as a cake!

David Orme

GREGORY GRUBER

Gregory Gruber, gargantuan glutton
would gobble green gooseberries, grumbo and mutton.
He'd gurgle down gravy, gulp garlic galore
then like a great gannet, would gullet some more.
'Oh, glorious grub,' he would gasp. 'Give me grease,
give me gobstoppers, gristle. (He gave us no peace.)
Give me gollops of gruel and gobbets of goose,
grill it and garnish it, glaze it. And juice,
give me gallons and gallons to gulp and to glug
and give it to me in a gardener's trug.'
Gregory Gruber grew gross as he guzzled.
Poor Gregory Gruber should've been muzzled
for that great gourmandister's gut overloaded
and Gregory Gruber (we warned him) exploded.

Marian Swinger

THERE WAS A YOUNG LADY OF RYDE

There was a young lady of Ryde,
Who ate some green apples and died.
The apples fermented
Inside the lamented,
And made cider inside her inside.

Anon.

GREEDYGUTS

I sat in the café and sipped at a Coke
There sat down beside me a WHOPPING great bloke
Who sighed as he elbowed me into the wall:
'Your trouble, my boy, is your belly's too small!
Your bottom's too thin! Take a lesson from me:
I may not be nice, but I'm GREAT, you'll agree,
And I've lasted a lifetime by playing this hunch:
The bigger the breakfast, the larger the lunch!

The larger the lunch, then the huger the supper.
The deeper the teapot, the vaster the cupper.
The fatter the sausage, the fuller the tea.
The MORE on the table, the BETTER for ME!'

His elbows moved in and his elbows moved out,
His belly grew bigger, chins wobbled about,
As forkful by forkful and plate after plate,
He ate and he ate and he ate and he ATE!

I hardly could breathe, I was squashed out of shape,
So under the table I made my escape.

'Aha!' he rejoiced, 'when it's put to the test,
The fellow who's fattest will come off the best!
Remember, my boy, when it comes to the crunch:
The bigger the breakfast, the larger the lunch!

The larger the lunch, then the huger the supper.
The deeper the teapot, the vaster the cupper.
The fatter the sausage, the fuller the tea.
The MORE on the table, the BETTER for ME!'

A lady came by who was scrubbing the floor
With a mop and a bucket. To even the score,
I lifted that bucket of water and said,
As I poured the whole lot of it over his head:

'*I've* found all my life, it's a pretty sure bet:
The FULLER the bucket, the WETTER you GET!'

Kit Wright

There was a young man called Strathspey
Who swallowed a pigeon one day.
He felt such a twerp
He made himself burp
And the pigeon flew out and away.

Michael Palin

TUMMY BUBBLE

A burp is just a bubble
that forms inside your tum.
But if it goes the other way,
say nothing, just play dumb.

Bruce Lamsky

On Nevski Bridge a Russian stood
Chewing his beard for lack of food.
Said he, 'It's tough this stuff to eat
But a darn sight better than shredded wheat!'

Anon.

SEND MY SPINACH

Send my spinach
Off to Spain.
Parcel post it
On a train.
Mail it,
Sail it,
On a ship.
Just don't let it
Touch my lip.

Douglas Florian

Alligator pie, alligator pie,
If I don't get some I think I'm gonna die.
Give away the green grass, give away the sky,
But don't give away my alligator pie.

Alligator stew, alligator stew,
If I don't get some I don't know what I'll do.
Give away my furry hat, give away my shoe,
But don't give away my alligator stew.

Alligator soup, alligator soup,
If I don't get some I think I'm gonna droop.
Give away my hockey stick, give away my hoop,
But don't give away my alligator soup.

Dennis Lee

JELLY JAKE AND BUTTER BILL

Jelly Jake and Butter Bill
One dark night when all was still
Pattered down the long, dark stair,
And no one saw the guilty pair;
Pushed aside the pantry door
And there found everything galore –
Honey, raisins, orange-peel,
Cold chicken aplenty for a meal,
Gingerbread enough to fill
Two such boys as Jake and Bill.
Well, they ate and ate and ate,
Gobbled at an awful rate
Till I'm sure they soon weighed more
Than double what they did before.
And then, it's awful, still it's true,
The floor gave way and they went through.
Filled so full they couldn't fight,
Slowly they sank out of sight.
Father, Mother, Cousin Ann,
Cook and nurse and furnace man
Fished in forty-dozen ways
After them, for twenty days;
But not a soul has chance to get
A glimpse or a glimmer of them yet.
And I'm afraid we never will –
Poor Jelly Jake and Butter Bill.

Leroy F. Jackson

Ackees, chapatties
Dumplins an nan,
Channa an rotis
Onion uttapam,
Masala dosa
Green callaloo
Bhel an samosa
Corn an aloo.
Yam an cassava
Pepperpot stew,
Rotlo an guava
Rice an tofu,
Puri, paratha
Sesame casserole,
Brown eggless pasta
And brown bread rolls.

Soya milked muesli,
Soya bean curd
Soya sweet sweeties
Soya's de word,
Soya bean margarine
Soya bean sauce,

What can mek medicine?
Soya of course.
Soya meks yogurt
Soya ice cream,
Or soya sorbet
Soya reigns supreme,
Soya sticks liqoriced
Soya salads
Try any soya dish
Soya is bad.

Plantain an tabouli
Cornmeal pudding
Onion bhajee
Wid plenty cumin,
Breadfruit an coconuts
Molasses tea
Dairy free omelettes
Very chilli
Gingerbread, nut roast
Sorrell, paw paw,
Cocoa an rye toast
I tek dem on tour,
Drinking cool maubi
Meks me feel sweet,
What was dat question now?

What do we eat?

Benjamin Zephaniah

SPAGHETTI

A plate heaped high
with spaghetti
all covered with tomato sauce
is just about my favourite meal.
It looks just like
a gigantic heap of:
steaming
                    tangled
          mixed
                    up
twizzled
                    twisted
wound
          up
                    woozled
WORMS!
I like picking them up
one at a time;
swallowing them slowly
head first,
until the tail flips
across my cheek
before finally wriggling
down my throat.

But best of all,
when I've finished eating
I go and look in a mirror
because the tomato sauce
smeared around my mouth
makes me look like a clown.

Frank Flynn

We sit down to eat
and the potato's a bit hot
so I only put a little bit on my fork
and I blow
whooph whooph
until it's cool
just cool
then into the mouth
nice.
And there's my brother
he's doing the same
whooph whooph
into the mouth
nice.
There's my mum
she's doing the same
whooph whooph
into the mouth
nice.

But my dad.
My dad.
What does he do?
He stuffs a great big chunk of potato
into his mouth
then
that really does it.
His eyes pop out
he flaps his hands
he blows, he puffs, he yells
he bobs his head up and down
he spits bits of potato
all over his plate
and he turns to us and says
'Watch out everybody –
the potato's very hot.'

Michael Rosen

AN 'EVERYTHING' PIZZA

I ordered an 'everything' pizza,
which probably was a mistake.
For it came with a bagful of doughnuts;
it came with a shovel and rake.
It came with a woman named Ida.
It came with a man from Peru.
It came with a half jar of peanuts.
It came with somebody's left shoe.
It came with a clown from the circus.
It came with a butterfly net.
It came with a small piece of Kleenex
that was used by Marie Antoinette.
It came with an open umbrella.
It came with some old smelly socks.
It came with a picture of Lassie,
and two lovely grandfather clocks.
It came with a nice set of dishes.
It came with a stale loaf of bread.
It came with a sack of potatoes.
It came with a four-poster bed.
It came with a dining room table.
It came with a washer and dryer.
It came with a broken guitar string.
It came with a radial tire.
It came with a golden retriever.
It came with a basket of fruit.

It came with a bottle of mustard.
It came with a red rubber boot.
It came with a college professor.
It came with a hive full of bees.
And then – this is simply amazing –
they forgot to put on any cheese!

Linda J. Knaus

KNOXVILLE, TENNESSEE

I always like summer
best
you can eat fresh corn
from daddy's garden
and okra
and greens
and cabbage
and lots of
barbecue
and buttermilk
and home-made ice cream
at the church picnic
and listen to
gospel music
outside
at the church
homecoming
and go to the mountains with
your grandmother
and go barefooted
and be warm
all the time
not only when you go to bed
and sleep

Nikki Giovanni

EATING WHILE READING

What is better
Than this book
And the churn of candy
In your mouth,
Or the balloon of bubble gum,
Or the crack of sunflower seeds,
Or the swig of soda,
Or the twist of beef jerky,
Or the slow slither
Of snow cone syrup
Running down your arms?

What is better than
This sweet dance
On the tongue,
And this book
that pulls you in?
It yells, *'Over here!'*
And you hurry along
With a red, sticky face.

Gary Soto

COWS

Half the time they munched the grass, and all the time
  they lay
Down in the water-meadows, the lazy month of May,
            A-chewing,
            A-mooing,
  To pass the hours away.

'Nice weather,' said the brown cow.
  'Ah,' said the white.
'Grass is very tasty.'
    'Grass is all right.'

Half the time they munched the grass, and all the time
  they lay
Down in the water-meadows, the lazy month of May,
            A-chewing,
            A-mooing,
  To pass the hours away.

'Rain coming,' said the brown cow.
'Ah,' said the white.
'Flies is very tiresome.'
    'Flies bite.'

Half the time they munched the grass, and all the time
  they lay
Down in the water-meadows, the lazy month of May,
            A-chewing,
            A-mooing,
  To pass the hours away.

'Time to go,' said the brown cow.
  'Ah,' said the white.
'Nice chat.' 'Very pleasant.'
  'Night.' 'Night.'

Half the time they munched the grass, and all the time
  they lay
Down in the water-meadows, the lazy month of May,
      A-chewing,
      A-mooing,
  To pass the hours away.

James Reeves

INDEX OF FIRST LINES

INDEX OF POETS

ACKNOWLEDGEMENTS

SENSATIONAL: POEMS INSPIRED BY THE FIVE SENSES

COMPILED BY

ROGER McGOUGH

The compiler and publishers wish to thank the following for permission to use copyright material:

John Agard, 'Mrs Skunk Writes a Letter to the Press' from *We Animals Would Like a Word With You* by John Agard, Bodley Head (1996), by permission of The Random House Group Ltd; **David Bateman**, 'Special Telescope', 'My Uncommon Senses' and 'Five Haiku For Five Senses'. Copyright © 2002, 1998 David Bateman, by permission of the author; **Connie Bensley**, 'Accountability' and 'Seeing Things' from *Central Reservations: New and Selected Poems* by Connie Bensley (1990), by permission of Bloodaxe Books; **James Berry**, 'Benediction'. Copyright © James Berry, by permission of The Peters Fraser and Dunlop Group Ltd on behalf of the author; **Margaret Wise Brown**, 'The Secret Song' from *Nibble Nibble* by Margaret Wise Brown. Copyright © 1959 by William R. Scott, Inc, renewed © 1987 by Roberta Brown Rauch, by permission of HarperCollins Publishers, Inc; **John Clare**, 'Pleasant Sounds'. Copyright © 1984 Eric Robinson, by permission of Curtis Brown Group Ltd, London on behalf of Eric Robertson; **Hilary Clough**, 'Silly Moo!', by permission of the author; **Mandy Coe**, 'Sensing Mother' and 'Shut Down', by permission of the author; **Billy Collins**, 'Another Reason Why I Don't Keep a Gun in the House' from *Taking off Emily Dickinson's Clothes* by Billy Collins, Picador, by permission of Macmillan, London; **John Cotton**, 'Only', from *Two by Two: Poems by John Cotton and Fred Sedgwick*, Tricky Sam! Press (1996), by permission of the Estate of the author; **W. H. Davies**, 'Leisure', by permission of Dee and Griffin, Solicitors, on behalf of the Estate of the author; **Peter Dixon**, 'The Colour of My Dreams' from *The Colour of My Dreams*, by Peter Dixon, Macmillan (2002), 'Lost Rainbow' from *The Penguin in the Fridge* by Peter Dixon, Macmillan (2001), and 'Before the Days of Noah', by permission of the author; **Berlie Doherty**, 'Quieter than Snow' from *Walking on Air* by Berlie Doherty, by permission of David Higham Associates on behalf of the author; **Carol Ann Duffy**, 'The Oldest Girl in the World' from *The Oldest Girl in the World* by Carol Ann Duffy, and 'Chocs' from *Meeting Midnight* by Carol Ann Duffy (1999), by permission of Faber and Faber Ltd; **Richard Edwards**, 'The Blue Room', by permission of the author; **T. S. Eliot**, 'Preludes' from *Collected Poems 1909–1962* by T. S. Eliot, by permission of Faber and Faber Ltd; **Eleanor Farjeon**, 'The Distance' from *Silver Sand and Snow* by Eleanor Farjeon, Michael Joseph, by permission of David Higham Associates on behalf of the author; **Max Fatchen**, 'Ears' from *Wry Rhymes for Troublesome Times* by Max Fatchen, Kestrel (1983), by permission of John Johnson Ltd on behalf of the author; **Vicki Feaver**, 'Crab Apple Jelly' from *The Handless Maiden* by Vicki Feaver, Jonathan Cape, by permission of The Random House Group Ltd; **Lawrence Ferlinghetti**, 'Fortune' from *The Coney Island of the Mind* by Lawrence Ferlinghetti. Copyright © 1958 by Lawrence Ferlinghetti, by permission of New Directions Publishing Corporation; **Douglas Florian**, 'Send My Spinach' from *Bing Bang Boing* by Douglas Florian. Copyright © 1994 by Douglas Florian, by permission of Harcourt, Inc; **Frank Flynn**, 'Spaghetti', by permission of the author; **Nikki Giovanni**, 'Knoxville, Tennessee', from *Black Feeling, Black Talk, Black Judgement* by Nikki Giovanni. Copyright © 1968, 1970

DRAGONS!

Fire-breathing poems by Nick Toczek

Prepare to be dazzled by all things dragon!

A wonderful collection starring these fascinating
mythical creatures by dragon connoisseur,
poet and magician Nick Toczek.
A lively, funny book packed with poems
that are perfect to read aloud.

The Magic of Dragons

Her pyrotechnics never fail.
She breathes on things. They burn, but they'll
Return unburned in just two ticks.
Dragon's doing magic tricks.

POEMS BY STEPHEN KNIGHT

Be tempted inside this quirky collection, packed full of
dark, delicious and delightful poems.

The World's Worst Escapologist

moved in next door to us last year.
Now, 254
milk bottles sit, unclaimed, outside his door.
I wonder why we haven't seen him yet.

'An intelligent collection of beautifully crafted poems'
Books for Keeps

A selected list of titles available from Macmillan Children's Books

The prices shown below are correct at the time of going to press. However, Macmillan Publishers reserves the right to show new retail prices on covers, which may differ from those previously advertised.

Sardines Poems by Stephen Knight	978-0-330-41356-5	£4.99
The Language of Love Poems chosen by Anne Harvey	978-0-330-41572-9	£4.99
Poems of Childhood Chosen by Brian Moses	978-0-330-41567-5	£4.99
Dragons! Poems by Nick Toczek	978-0-330-43744-8	£4.99

All Pan Macmillan titles can be ordered from our website, www.panmacmillan.com, or from your local bookshop and are also available by post from:

Bookpost, PO Box 29, Douglas, Isle of Man IM99 1BQ
Credit cards accepted. For details:
Telephone: 01624 677237
Fax: 01624 670923
Email: bookshop@enterprise.net
www.bookpost.co.uk

Free postage and packing in the United Kingdom